eat

eat.shop.brooklyn. *first edition*

eat.shop.brooklyn was researched, written and photographed by agnes baddoo
the eat.shop.guides were created by kaie wellman

as a child of manhattan my love affair with brooklyn began with visits to my great-grandmother in fort greene. as an adult i couldn't resist the borough, so i shared a brownstone on bergen street in boerum hill with a group of friends. at the time i was in a band called the bushmills (after our drink of choice) that formed spontaneously on our stoop. i refer to the bushmills and those fine days often in this guide. as you can imagine, brooklyn was a different world then (in the late 1980's). dumbo and williamsburg, now percolating hotbeds of activity, were barely residential and virtually uninhabited. during this time i met kaie, who is the creator of the *eat.shop.guides*. she would come in from l.a. and hang with the bergen street crew, and it was here that we began our long-friendship. there has been many a good meal and shopping tip shared between us.

though some believe that kaie began these guides so she could travel the country eating and shopping, the truth is that she wanted to seek out and champion local, independently owned businesses that define the cities in which we live. the first *eat.shop.guide* was published in portland, oregon the winter of 2003 and now two years later i am authoring the first east coast book.

and my credentials? since my days in a stroller every shopping excursion with my mother had a tasty treat as it's ultimate destination. actually it was more like a bribe. if my mother wanted to hit the bloomingdale's white sale, zum zum's was promised as the prize for good behavior. so that's how every store, every neighborhood became distinguished for me: by it's eating and shopping potential. as you can see, i was born to write this guide.

as brooklyn is massive, i don't presume to represent the entire borough with 88 featured businesses. the goal instead is to be a filter, and highlight some of the extraordinary and unique businesses. with this as a touchpoint, you can take the time to explore each neighborhood – there's a vast amount to discover.

for residents of nyc, i hope that you'll discover places you haven't come across before, and rediscover the places you already love. for visitors, by getting to know these neighborhoods by the unique places that define them, you will get an incredible sense of brooklyn.

agnes baddoo
25 august 2005

tips on using the guide and exploring brooklyn

1 > explore from neighborhood to neighborhood. note that almost every neighborhood i have featured has dozens of great stores and restaurants other than my favorites.

2 > make sure to double check the hours of the establishment before you visit. sometimes the businesses change their hours seasonally.

3 > the pictures and descriptions of each business are representational. please don't be distraught when the business no longer carries or is not serving something you saw or read about in the guide.

4 > although the subway is the easiest method of getting around brooklyn, i suggest you pick up a brooklyn bus map at the 'token booth' in a train station. you'll get a better lay of the land – how the neighborhoods connect and overlap and you'll also get to see more above ground and therefore be better oriented

5 > if you're coming over from manhattan, the main subway lines into brooklyn are: f / b / d / q / a / c / m / n / r / 2 / 3 / 4 / 5 which gives you a good number of choices.

6 > back to the buses: the b61 bus is a joyride. it goes from williamsburg through the brooklyn navy yards, dumbo, downtown, atlantic avenue to the columbia street waterfront and red hook. in fact the b61 is the only form of public transportation to reach the waterfront and red hook.

7 > remember, use the maps to give you a sense of each neighborhood, but note that they are not to scale.

8 > have a good time.

eat

shop

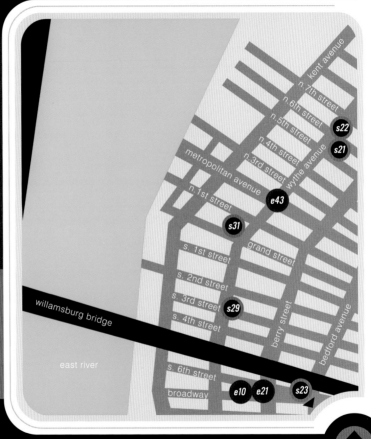

williamsburg

williamsburg

m2

eat

shop

s14 city joinery
s24 halcyon the shop
s44 wonk

east river

john street

pearl street

plymouth street

s14

s24

water street

manhattan bridge

s44

front street

adams street

jay street

bridge street

york street

brooklyn queens expressway

dumbo

eat

e3 staubitz market

e5 bedoin tent

e9 d'amico foods

e26 sahadi's

e27 sal's pizzeria

e37 the grocery

e40 tuller premium food

shop

S2 acorn

S5 area yoga & baby

s10 butter

s18 darr

s20 flirt

s23 grdn

s26 layla

s35 refinery

s40 swallow

s43 watts on smith

brooklyn heights | cobble hill | boerum hill | carroll gardens

m4

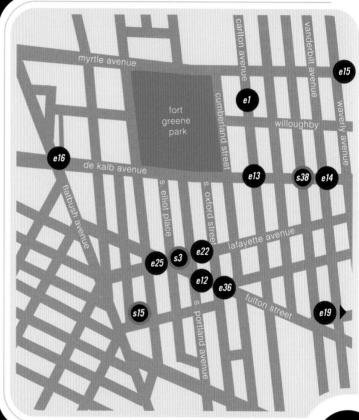

downtown | clinton hill | prospect heights | fort greene

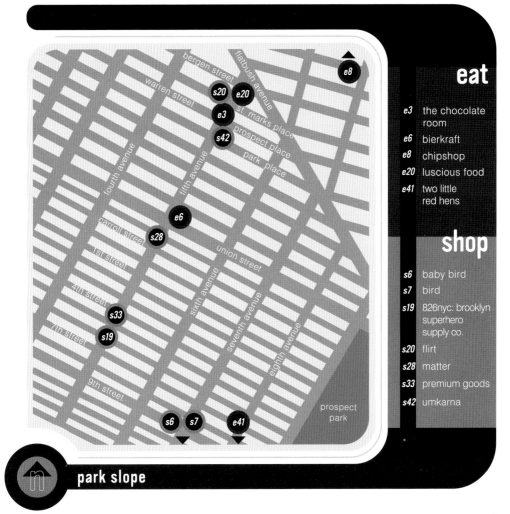

eat

e3 the chocolate room

e6 bierkraft

e8 chipshop

e20 luscious food

e41 two little red hens

shop

s6 baby bird

s7 bird

s19 826nyc: brooklyn superhero supply co.

s20 flirt

s28 matter

s33 premium goods

s42 umkarna

park slope

m6

eat

e3 alma
e8 brooklyn collective
e28 schnack

shop

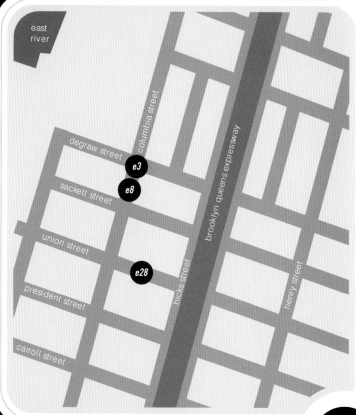

east river

degraw street

columbia street

brooklyn queens expressway

sackett street

union street

hicks street

president street

henry street

carroll street

e3
e8
e28

columbia street waterfront district

eat

e18 lenell's
e32 steve's authentic key lime pie
e39 360

shop

red hook

m8

eat

e4 banana leaf

shop

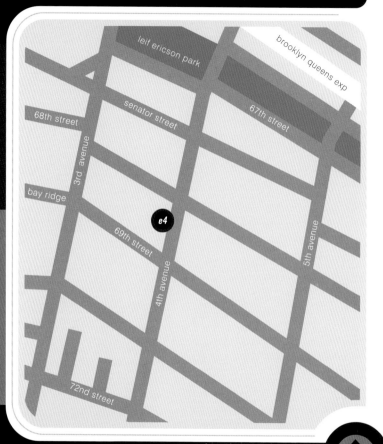

leif ericson park

brooklyn queens exp

68th street

senator street

67th street

3rd avenue

bay ridge

e4

69th street

5th avenue

4th avenue

72nd street

bay ridge

eat

e17 la brioche expresso
e24 odessa

shop

brighton beach

m10

a bistro

164 carlton avenue. between willoughby and myrtle. (c/f) (laf. jay)
718.855.9255
m-tu closed. w - sa. 5.30pm - 11pm. su - su 11.00am - 4pm

senegalese cuisine
opened in 2005. chef: abdoul gueye
owners: abdoul and cassandra gueye
$$: all major credit cards accepted
dinner. brunch. reservations recommended

in los angeles, my friend from senegal, aziz, has shared many a delectable meal with friends around a large platter of jolloff rice, tieboudienne, and on and on. these are invitations not to be missed. senegalese food is familiar yet different. think louisiana cuisine with different spices and hold the roux, plus it's not as heavy. at *a bistro,* you can feel the love and you can taste the magic of chef abduol's simple, elegant and delicious food. everybody's happy.

imbibe:
bissop
la mamba

devour:
senegalese fried chicken
crab cake
abdoul's mussels
quinoa salad
sorrel & ginger créme brûlée

acqua santa

all italian
opened in 2000. chef / owner: mariano lamanno
$$: all major credit cards accepted
lunch. dinner. brunch. wine and beer. reservations recommended

> **e2**

during the dog days of n.y. summer, the humidity will drive you to delusions. at *acqua santa,* one delusion i can indulge in is that i am in some faraway seaside italian trattoria enjoying the breezes, dining *al fresco* in a large patio shaded by grape leaves. i drink the homemade limoncello, eat the divine classic salad of arugula, shaved parmesan, lemon, olive oil and perfectly cooked bacon (made my way with large pieces) and marvel at life's simple pleasures.

imbibe:
homemade limoncello
mimosa with fresh orange juice & prosecco

devour:
herb & tomato focaccia
delicious thin crust pizza
whole wheat linguine with veggies
pork tenderloin baked with apples & sherry
spiedino

alma

oaxacan cuisine
opened in 2002. owners: ron starns and anthony capone
$$: all major credit cards accepted
dinner. brunch. full bar. happy hour at b61 bar. first come, first served

> *e3*

after a browse at *freebird books*, i wandered down to *alma* for some libation and sustenance oaxacan style. i arrived on a balmy evening, in time for sunset cocktails on the rooftop deck. what a view! what a drink! *alma* is three floors of heart and soul. on the ground floor is the friendly neighborhood bar *b61*. the second floor dining room features wraparound windows and beautiful handcrafted woodwork; every bench, chair, table and windowsill has been crafted with love and good vibes by jamie and matt.

imbibe:
honeydew melon margarita
pomegranate martini

devour:
mole poblano de pollo
camarones asados
ceviche pescado
arroz con queso
slice of steve's authentic key lime pie

banana leaf

malaysian and thai cuisine
opened in 2003. chef: peter how. owners: peter how and lai heng to
$$: all credit cards accepted
lunch. dinner. reservations recommended

> **e4**

a little farther out than the other listings, bay ridge is beginning to percolate, and chef peter's *banana leaf* greets you when you emerge from the subway. this is one fine dining experience; one delicacy after another. he has combined the best of malaysian and thai – spicy but not too hot, crisp and fresh with warm and savory. refresh with a lychee drink and finish with coconut pineapple mousse. go with friends so you can try everything. otherwise, you just might be tempted to graze from the other tables.

imbibe:
malaysian iced tea
chrysanthemum ice drink

devour:
roti canai
green papaya salad
crispy soft shell crab
coconut seafood
rack of lamb with tamarind sticky rice

11

bedouin tent

middle eastern cuisine
opened in 1989. chef / owner: mohammad moustafa
$: cash only
lunch. dinner. brunch. first come, first served

> e5

sixteen years on atlantic avenue, this is another favorite takeout /eat-in spot from my living on bergen era. then it was *mr. moustache*, now it's *bedouin tent*. the pita's still handmade, baked on the spot and puffed up like a helium balloon – the perfect conveyor for hummus, tabouleh and baba ganouj. most importantly, the lambajin is as delicious as it was then, so i am extra happy. i like it when my memory and reality agree.

imbibe:
mint tea
turkish coffee

devour:
lambajin
falafel
handmade, freshly baked pita
baba ganouj
tabouleh

13

bierkraft

gourmet grocery and beer emporium
opened in 2001. owners: daphne and richard scholz
$$: all major credit cards accepted

> *e6*

just because you're not supposed to mix the grape with the grain doesn't mean the cheese has to pick sides. everything you need to know about which beers or which cheeses you can ask or discover for yourself at weekly themed complimentary tastings. there is a mesmerizing variety of both at *bierkraft* and the tastings are paired to contrast or complement — you decide. while mulling over these flavors, browse the grocery and find a new salt to bring home.

imbibe:
saison dupont
ayinger celebrator
goose island ipa
southampton imperial porter

devour:
250 artisanal cheeses
hormone & antibiotic-free meat
housemade organic duck leg confit

bozu

296 grand street. between roebling and havemeyer. brooklyn, ny
718.384.7770. www.bozu.com
sushi. small plates. sake bombs. sangria

japanese tapas bar
opened in 2004. chef: makoto suzuki
owners: shinji mizutani and makoto suzuki
$$: mc. visa
dinner. late night. full bar. reservations recommended on weekends

nibbles, nibbles, nibbles. some days you want to sit down to a hearty meal. on days like this it's the only way to refuel the weary machine. other daysthough only a cavalcade of tasty morsels will do the job. well, strike up the taiko and let the procession of japanese tapas begin. *bozu* is the perfect spot for a little ceviche, some shrimp kataifi, and a corps of 'bombs' (small, round decorative sushi). the food here will thrill your taste buds. to quote my friend bennett, "make food, not war!"

imbibe:
homemade infused shochu:
  grapefruit, persimmon, pomegranate & lychee
yuzu ranbutan martinis

devour:
salmon scallop & avocado ceviche
bombs
pork betty
shrimp kataifi

chipshop

english pub
opened in 2001. chef: ashamsu hagan
owners: christopher sell and bobby gagnon
$$: atlantic: accepts all major credit cards. 5th: cash only
lunch. dinner. brunch. late night. full bar. first come, first served

> **e8**

america seems to go through food crazes. remember the ice cream wars? burrito bonanza? fresh pasta mania? suddenly sushi everywhere? these days i detect english pub fever in the air. fish and chips, bangers and mash, a well-portioned, full english breakfast all done like they do on the british isles. and yes there's fizzy ribena and toast soldiers for dipping. i think it's more elvis than english but believe me when i say: you've haven't lived until you try *chipshop's* fried twinkie.

imbibe:
fizzie ribena
bucks fizz

devour:
hangover special
fish & chips
bangers & mash
boiled eggs with toast soldiers
fried twinkie

d'amico foods

fresh roasted coffee and family-owned deli
opened in 1948. owner: frank jr. d'amico
$: all major credit cards accepted

> **e9**

my father is from ghana, my grandmother from jamaica – two places where coffee is king. i had a college inter-term job in the coffee department of the short-lived delaurentis emporium because i love the smell of coffee beans roasting. *d'amico's* is coffee bean aroma therapy – there's continuous roasting all day long! stand in front of the handsome industrial-era roaster or grinder and breath deeply. face the opposite direction, and order the most perfect sandwich from the deli. old world charm lives!

imbibe:
hot cup of redhook blend coffee
90 plus varieties of coffee blends
granita

devour:
d'amico brand olive oils & vinegars
prosciutto, sharp provolone &
   olivada on a small roll

21

diner

simple, delicious basics with excellent specials
opened in 1999. chef: caroline fidanza. owners: andrew tarlow and mark firth
$$: all major credit cards accepted
lunch. dinner. brunch. late night. full bar. first come, first served

> _e10_

i first came to *diner* last summer after a day in long beach. a group of sun-and-sea-weary friends navigated the subway and the stroll to the restaurant and piled into a back booth for the meal we'd all been dreaming of. it started with beers and mint juleps, progressed to mussels, perfect burgers, grilled fish, sautéed greens and pork chops. forks were flying. no matter how much we enjoyed our own order it was imperitive that we sampled each other's, save for the flourless chocolate cake. that was just too hard to share.

imbibe:
the blood orange cosmo
the rosemary salty dog

devour:
mussels with fries
grilled scallops with corn, mint &
    cucumber salad
whole dorade with string beans
flourless chocolate cake

dumont

american seasonal cuisine
opened in 2001. chefs: polo dobkin and cal elliott. owner: colin devlin
$$: mc. visa
brunch. lunch. dinner. first come, first served

> *e11*

named after the original fourth network and tv brand, *dumont* serves up hearty american seasonal classics with a flair. last summer, when i was staying on devoe street i had the convenience and pleasure of having to pass or enter *dumont* on my way home (i chose enter). warm light, wood benches, outdoor garden treehouse dining, the cozy drinks detention room — it's all very inviting. but everyone knows the real lure is their mac and cheese for all seasons. coming soon: *dumont* burger and late night takeout.

imbibe:
the pomegranate martini
the makers sidecar

devour:
mac & cheese
pan-roasted quail
grilled scallops with frisee, orange,
    grapefruit & gold beets
seared tuna with fingerling potatoes

habana outpost: brooklyn

new york's only solar-powered cuban-mexican restaurant
opened in 2005. chef: oscar teco. owner: sean meenan
$: cash only
dinner. full bar. first come, first served

> *e12*

on mid-summer evenings, new yorkers head outside. *habana outpost* is pretty much all outside. a corner lot with vibrantly painted walls, picnic tables, a glider swing, mexican fountains and an outfitted kitchen truck where oscar cooks cuban and mexican hits. families, couples, friends are eating, drinking, chilling. sunday night it's classic movies projected above the solar panels; weekends it's a flea market. beyond this sense of community, the agenda here is a thriving green business. lead by example and have fun doing so!

imbibe:
jarrito sodas
brooklyn draft beer

devour:
mexican corn on the cob
cuban sandwiches
chicken diablo sandwiches
veggie dogs
mango salad

i-shebeen madiba

south african restaurant and bar
opened in 1999. chef: armando soltero. owner: mark henegan
$$: all major credit cards accepted
breakfast. lunch. dinner. brunch. full bar. reservations recommended

> **e13**

in south africa, *madiba* is an affectionate nickname for nelson mandela. i am full of affection for this vibrant neighborhood vortex. it's one of my first stops when i get to town. through delicious food, welcoming staff, fun drinks and excellent music, *i-shebeen madiba* realizes all that mandela has come to represent: all ages, all cultures, neighbors and strangers meeting, mixing, eating, drinking, dancing, wedding — it's all going on at *madiba*. after one visit you, too, will feel local.

imbibe:
the *i-shebeen* queen
mojitos served in mason jars

devour:
fish parcel wrapped in newspaper
grilled prawns with yellow rice
pap boerwors
i-shebeen salad daily special
malva pudding

ici

organic french bistro
opened in 2004.   chef: julie e. farias   owner: laurent saillard
$$: all major credit cards
breakfast. lunch. dinner. brunch. beer and wine.   reservations recommended

> **e14**

laurent seems to be the "no degree of separation" man, the nexus lexus of the new generation of great brooklyn restaurateurs. "when you go here, say hello to so and so, we were at such and such restaurant together," he'll say. at his bright organic french bistro *ici*, you'll be met with warm welcomes and cuisine that is imaginatively combined and beautifully presented. simple, delectable elegance. i still dream of the refreshing frozen lemon basil sake drink. vivre les artichauds! vivre les courgettes! a notre sante!

imbibe:
blood orange iced tea
frozen lemon basil sake

devour:
fluke carpaccio
farm chicken with orange couscous
wide stripe bass with onion
   & tomato confit
honey yogurt panna cotta

jive turkey

the first retailer of its kind in nyc to specialize in whole fried trukey
opened in 2003. owner: aricka westbrooks
$: all major credit cards accepted
lunch. dinner. first come, first served

> *e15*

for a few years i didn't make it home for thanksgiving. nothing i ate in its stead would satisfy me. i'd spend the rest of the year searching in vain for a good turkey dinner. thanks to aricka, culinary dilemma solved. at *jive turkey* i can have an individual or whole deep-fried turkey dinner, all the trimmings (with a southern/caribbean accent for good measure) any day of the week. in 28 blessed states a turkey delivery can even come accompanied with a specially selected wine courtesy of *the greene grape*. for this i am truly thankful.

imbibe:
ginger mint lemonade

devour:
turkey chili
the gobbler salad with turkey, walnuts, blue
    cheese, croutons & dried cranberries
whole fried turkey in 15 different flavors
fried turkey sandwich
traditional bread pudding

33

junior's

legendary family owned and operated restaurant
opened in 1950. chefs: adam marks and joseph hanson
owners: kevin and alan rosen
$: all major credit cards
breakfast. lunch. dinner. brunch. late night. full bar. first come, first served

> *e16*

along with the old williamsburg bank tower, *junior's* is one of brooklyn's most famous landmarks. everyone knows those flashing lights. and everyone knows the cheesecake. be it breakfast, lunch or dinner, it's all about the cheesecake. politicians have been known to hop off the campaign trail for a slice. from the counter to the booths, to the dining room in the dark and moody cocktail lounge, it's full of vibes and history. its always hopping here morning, noon and night.

imbibe:
junior's skyscraper ice cream float
fox's u bet brooklyn egg cream

devour:
corned beef & pastrami delux
"d" burger
individual meatloaf
original cheesecake

35

la brioche expresso

russian / french bakery
opened in 1990. chef: helen sobolevsky. owner: peter sobolevsky
$: all major credit cards accepted
breakfast. brunch. first come, first served

> *e17*

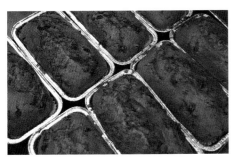

it's 87 degrees, with 90 percent humidity. the only thing to do is head to water. claudia, her son elias and i make our way to brighton beach. claudia and i met when we were three, in a tree in central park. hardly a summer has passed that didn't involve some summer-in-the-city adventures. with the boardwalk ahead and the coney island '"water flume" as our destination, elias, a natural explorer, leads us to *la brioche* because we'll need pastries and sweets for our adventure!

imbibe:
cappucinos
espressos

devour:
mocha creme cake
russian rausch babka
piroshki
savory sandwiches
helen's famous sour cream cake

lenell's

wine and spirit boutique
opened in 2003. owner: lenell smothers
$. all major credit cards accepted

> *e18*

lenell brings her dry southern wit to her love of wines and spirits. there's nothing stuffy, uptight or pretentious about her or the wide variety of novel and exceptional products. for her weekend gin symposium, an assortment of uncommon brands are artfully assembled in a claw foot tub. like books in a quirky bookstore, the wines are grouped by subject – the dog or cat labels together, lady vintners together. but mostly, it's her straight-shootin', "don't bring none, won't be none" attitude that makes *lenell's* a fixture in red hook.

imbibe:
large bourbon selection
genever gins
pappy van winkle bourbon
english mead
rittenhouse rye
edouardo valentini wines

locanda vini & olii

northern italian home cooking
opened in 2001. chef: catherine de zagon
owners: francois louy and catherine de zagon
$$: mc. visa
dinner. reservations recommended on weekend

> *e19*

this place was a recommendation from many friends, and when i read the menu, my heart skipped a beat. i immediately had to call kaie (who was married in piemonte) to read passages. this was food lust. the simple northern italian combinations listed are so mouth-watering they are almost obscene. *vini & olii* is a culinary love fest. françois and catherine, who rescued a 130-year-old pharmacy to house *vini* in, make well-portioned multi-course offerings as if you were at a loved one's home in italy. now that's *amore*.

imbibe:
rosso in bottiglia
chinotto & bitters

devour:
charcuterie from the sea
homemade pastas
piedmontese beef from montana
branzino
chocolate almond torte

luscious food

gourmet deli
opened in 2005. chef: christine zeni
owners: christine zeni and stacy mooradian
$$: all major credit cards accepted
breakfast. lunch. dinner. brunch. first come, first served

> *e20*

luscious and *food*, now those are two words i like together. when you walk into the deli, from the way they make their sandwiches and prepared foods to the carefully chosen groceries, you know christine and stacy love everything about food. i don't mean they are foodies, but food lovers. when they say, "eat passionately," we listen. people come back again and again for their favorite soup, sandwich (slow roasted beef, anyone?), salad or for coffee with homemade chocolate pecan cookies.

imbibe:
teany teas
gus grown-up sodas

devour:
slow-roasted beef sandwich
cuban mojo with slow-roasted pork loin
  & gruyere on ciabatta
luscious salad
homemade chocolate chip-pecan cookies

marlow & sons

oyster bar and local grocery
opened in 2005. chef: caroline fidanza. owners: andrew tarlow and mark firth
$$: all major credit cards accepted
lunch. dinner. brunch. late night. oyster happy hour
first come, first served

> *e21*

full of good ideas, andrew and mark of *diner* opened a grocery store and oyster bar right around the corner. *marlow & sons* carries produce from small farms, all kinds of hard-to-find delicacies, condiments, breads, candies, chips and jerky. but wait, there's more in back, where there's a rustic french-style bar with wood paneling, long tables, round tables, benches, chairs and a full bar. order up a dozen oysters and a glass of rosé. what more do you want? well, maybe a set of keys and a cot.

imbibe:
oyster bar happy hour
excellent rosé wine list

devour:
locally grown produce
soft-shell crabs
charcuteries
east & west coast oysters

moe's

bar / lounge
opened in 2001. owners: ruby lawrence and chelsea altman
$: cash only
full bar. happy hour. first come, first served

> *e22*

my goddaughter, kanya, went to pratt, and *moe's* is still one of her favorite spots. so i went. what is it about fort greene? it's just one good vibe spot after another. though differing in decor each place is homey and familiar. *moe's* was packed on the sunday night i went, with a band playing in the back living room. as soon as ruby, the owner, and i were introduced, our childhoods scrolled before our eyes. talk about familiar – i was her camp counselor assistant many summers ago! hugs and rounds all around!

imbibe:
the ruby tuesday
the lafayette
the little france
the ft. green
the pirate

moto

simple, delicious food
opened in 2002. owners: bill phelps and john maccormack
$$: cash only
dinner. brunch. first come, first served

> *e23*

when more than four store or restaurant owners refer you to a restaurant, you know something special is going on. located on the outer fringe of williamsburg, *moto* is a corner building with a corner entrance. the warmly lit room draws you directly to the u-shaped bar where you orient yourself with a black velvet. every inch of this space was gutted and built from scratch, so there's much to take in. the food is amazingly well-priced, simple, innovative and plate-licking delicious. go now.

imbibe:
corsendonk on tap
black velvet (guiness & champagne)

devour:
panini
rotisserie pork ribs with herbs de provence
mash & greens
louisiana shrimp boil
warm date cake with toffee sauce & cream

odessa

russian-american delicatessen
opened in 1982. chef: manel cherdak. owner: alexander balagula
$: all major credit cards accepted
first come, first served

> *e24*

looking for caviar? chicken kiev? kvas natural sodas? *odessa* is your culinary gateway to the ukraine. with sturgeon, langoustine, every kind of dairy product, sausage and pickles. from groceries to prepared foods, this deli is well stocked with many treats. those in the know make the trek to brighton beach, and those in the neighborhood are very satisfied. create a picnic of russian potato salad, grilled veggies, some kabobs and duchesse pear soda. make your way to the to the boardwalk, it's just a couple of blocks away .

imbibe:
borjoini georgian water
baltic beer

devour:
sturgeon
chicken kiev
langoustines
chicken kabobs
beef, pork, chicken & veal sausages

restaurant gia

american cuisine with many influences
opened in 2003. chef / owner: ian grant
$$: all major credit cards accepted
dinner. brunch. reservations recommended

> *e25*

restaurant gia is so sleek you almost pass the modern façade. inside, that sleekness continues from the chic bar and lounge to the stark dining room upstairs. very cosmopolitan. after a long day, sit at the bar, have a *gia*tini and leave work behind. order a little tide-me-over from the bar menu. for me, a mini brioche burger with grilled onions is the mouth-watering definition of american cuisine. there is attention to detail, ingredients and presentation – you can see that ian enjoys constructing visually elegant taste sensations.

imbibe:
the *gia*tini
the chocolatini

devour:
nori crusted & seared yellowfin tuna
mini *gia* burgers on toasted brioche
quinoa salad with jicama, arugula, aged
    pecorino di vino & tomato vinaigrette
carrot cake

53

sahadi's

specialty and fine foods
opened in 1948. owners: charlie and robert sahadi
$$: all major credit cards accepted

> *e26*

sahadi's is the premier middle eastern market. opened in 1948, it is a pillar of the community and certainly an anchor of atlantic avenue. it boasts more than 30 types of olives, dried fruits, nuts, coffee beans, flat breads, crackers, toasts, and a staggering variety of oils, fetas and prepared foods – where to begin? try not to wander in hungry without a clue or you'll break the bank. if you have a list, try not to digress. besides the assortment of things i am familiar with, there are still so many things to try.

imbibe:
egyptian juices
pomegranate juice

devour:
30 olive varieties
oils, nuts, dried fruits, spices & salts
all the world's flatbreads & crackers
halva with pistachios
fried cauliflower from the deli

sal's pizzeria

pizzeria old style
opened in 1957. chef / owner: john esposito
$: cash only
dinner. late night. first come, first served

> *e27*

this was a favorite spot when three out of our members of my band, the bushmills, lived on bergen street. in those days some members of the compound went to the gym at the st. george. for some of us, exercise was limited to chasing down the ice cream truck or taking a slow stroll up to *sal's* for a plain slice served on paper with a coke. after, an italian ice and maybe a movie. happily, some things remain as i remember, with nice additions like rice balls and potato croquettes.

imbibe:
coca-cola
brooklyn lager on tap

devour:
classic slice
sliced sausage & broccoli rabe pizza
mini fried calzone
potato croquette
rice balls

schnäck

burger joint with great sausages
opened in 2002.   chef / owner: harry hawk
$: cash only
lunch. dinner. first come, first served

> e28

one rainy sunday evening i was with my friend bennett visiting from l.a. when i told him we were going to *schnäck* his reply was, "cool, I saw it on *cookin' in brooklyn*." sometimes i crave a cheeseburger, fries and a sundae but don't have time for the nap after. *schnäck's* solution: tiny single burgers with fries and soda combos. then you have enough room for a sundae too, and you don't need a nap. besides being totally kid friendly in menu, portions and decor, *schnäck* shops locally for ingredients. local food for local people.

imbibe:
boylan root beer float
dfh chicory stout

devour:
swojska sausage
single schnäckie combo
mexican corn
tofu reuben
choc. brownie schnäck style

59

spike hill

contemporary irish-american pub
opened in 2004. chef: brett ackerman. owner: tom kenny
$$: all major credit cards accepted
lunch. dinner. brunch. late night. full bar. happy hour. first come, first served

> *e29*

when i first peeked into *spike hill*, i stood in awe in front of the wall o' whiskey (my band wasn't called the bushmills for nothing!). i like whiskey like some people like wine, and i've only seen a selection this staggering on the british isles. dark, friendly, chatty, this place has an authentic pub vibe with a steady stream of quality entrées, re-worked bar snacks (nachos with a nearly drinkable dip) and an award-winning guiness pour – the best in nyc! and of course, the irish fry-up will surely cure whatever ails you...

imbibe:
guinness
ardbeg 27-year-old scotch

devour:
pork chops
irish fry-up
fish & chips
special salad
life-changing polenta

61

st. helen cafe

delicious, laid-back neighborhood vortex
opened in 2003. chef: noel hennessy
owners: noel hennessy, sean mcnanny and jeremy mcmillon $: cash only
breakfast. lunch. dinner. brunch. first come, first served

> *e30*

this place is everybody's favorite sanctuary. a tranquil place to chill, enjoy good food or coffee, then chill some more. during my many adventures in williamsburg, i'd stop in to regroup. from the misty blown-up photos of lakeside tall trees or the reflection pool in the lush garden, *st. helen* is calming. besides salads, practically everything is baked or toasted. thank god i am already sitting down when they serve me baked fontina with toasted focaccia strips and raw apples slices! mmm!

imbibe:
homemade fresh mint lemonade
seattle style coffee

devour:
avocado toast
baked fontina with garlic cloves
baked fruits with goat cheese
baked eggs with smoked salmon
chocolate croissant bread pudding

63

staubitz market

classic butcher
opened in 1917. owners: john mcfadden sr. and john mcfadden jr.
$$: mc. visa

> *e31*

in my humble opinion, a neighborhood is not a neighborhood without a butcher. not just any butcher, but a great, charming, meat-knowing, meat-loving butcher. one that knows what's best to do with any cut. all hail *staubitz*! the store opened in 1917; john sr.'s had it since 1950. he and his son john are everything and more when it comes to fine butchers. when i lived on bergen street, i'd walk over. when i was in williamsburg, i took the g train. i was not alone. many devoted people also make the trek for quality products and pleasantries.

devour:
aged prime beef
domestic & imported specialty cheeses
stonewall kitchen products
imported french lollipops
game >
  bison & venison
fowl >
  poussin, squab, quail & goose

steve's authentic key lime pie

fresh-squeezed key lime pie bakery
opened in 1995. owner: steve tarpin
$: all credit cards accepted, but cash is king
delivery

> **e32**

what's cookin' in brooklyn you ask? in red hook it's a lot of key lime pie. picture this: the day was steamy. young elias ran us through the sprinklers then my friend carolina led the way past a garden to a painted sign that read: "pies here" and off she rode. floridian steve greeted me like a long-lost friend. we talked pies, parenting, music, tales of the keys, even mangoes as a miami-style storm came and went. *steve's authentic key lime pies* are a little bit o' citrus magic available right here on pier 41 and coast to coast.

devour and support:
key lime pie tart
frozen chocolate dipped key lime slice
fresh key limes by the pound
the express: steve's '50s ford
    delivery truck. look for it, say hi!
portside, n.y.'s commitment to nurture
    the economic connection between
    people ashore and those on water

surf shack

surf shack, seafood restaurant and bar
opened in 2002. chef: freddy valencia. owner: maya pizzati
$: cash only
lunch. dinner. brunch. late night. full bar. happy hour
first come, first served

> *e33*

there's sand on the floor from the first step in the *surf shack* to the back garden, surfboards everywhere, and early jimmy cliff playing. we could be anywhere from tortola to oahu, save for 'the worms' album cover in the mix of photos on the wall. new yorkers of a certain era recognize simon, the bar sinister. save your frequent-flier miles because you can meet maya (and often simon) for early morning surf sessions, followed by the city's best lobster roll and a tiki drink or two.

imbibe:
the mojito
tiki drinks

devour:
chowder
legendary lobster roll
fish burrito
lobster with corn on the cob
chocolate soufflé

tainted lady lounge

cocktail lounge / bar
opened in 2004. owner: deb parker
$: all major credit cards
dinner. brunch. full bar. happy hour. late night. first come, first served

> **e34**

here's the scene at the *tainted lady lounge*: strong colorful drinks, great '50s & '60s rythym-and-blues playin', punk-a-billy records spinnin' and an extensive collection of saucy photos and paintings of naturally well-endowed women from by gone eras hangin'. with almost three dozen titillating libations to choose from, like the lizzie borden, the frances farmer or the veronica lake, you'll feel like you have stepped right out of a russ meyer movie.

imbibe:
the lizzie borden (extreme bloody mary)
the frances farmer (a zombie)
the veronica lake (a stinger)
the mae west (a red kiss)

devour:
burger debauchery: beef, turkey or
  free-range chicken breast
steve's authentic key lime pie

the chocolate room

the chocolate emergency center dessert cafe
opened in 2005. chefs: annastacia weiss and margaret hastings
owner: jon payson and naomi josepher
$$: mc. visa
first come, first served

> *e35*

the chocolate room is a brasserie featuring everything chocolate. the look may be brasserie, but i see more old world pharmacy filling chocolate prescriptions for whatever ails you. today i feel ganache-rolled-in-nuts deficient so i come here for my medicine. i suggest beginning with biscotti while you contemplate what you'll devour: cupcake or fondue? chocolate layer cake with bonny doon framboise or a chewy chocolate chip cookie with refreshing strawberry honey sorbet? hmmm, decisions, decisions, decisions...

imbibe:
bittersweet hot chocolate
banana hot chocolate

devour:
fresh mint-chip ice cream
chocolate cupcakes
chocolate fondue
valrhona molten chocolate cake
chocolate sorbet

the greene grape

765 fulton street between south portland and south oxford (718) 797 9463
11217 wine www.thegreenegrape.com
m-w 10pm th-f 11am 10pm sa 10am 10pm su 11am 8pm

wine (and some spirits) store
opened in 2004. owners: jason, sara and matt richelson
$$: all major credit cards accepted
wine tasting

fort greene > **e36**

i don't know much about wine, but i know what i like when i taste it. siblings jason, sara and matt take great pride in their thoughtful offerings at *the greene grape*. they deal with small family-owned producers and make the effort to help the wine novice find his or her own voice while satisfying and inspiring many a connoisseur. the store has a wonderful open feel to it, which makes the evening wine tastings very relaxing. drop in; it's like the wine-learning annex.

imbibe:
nieddera 2002 rosso valletirso contini
chateau calissane cuvée du chateau 2004
les collines 2003 côtes du rhône
la firande côtes du rhône
bruichladdich islay single malt
st. george single malt

the grocery

green-market driven, seasonal american
opened in 1999. chef / owners: sharon pachter and charles kiely
$$$: mc. visa
dinner. reservations recommended

> e37

if a picture paints a thousand words then there's little more i have to say about this acclaimed restaurant. from the cool gray interior to the wait staff poised at attention when you enter, you know you'll be going through some exacting culinary paces before the night is through. here's the news: beyond the beautifully presented delicacies, charles has created the ultimate granola bar. soft, dense, flavorful and not too sweet – reminds me of my grandma wallace's coconut bread. and coming soon: *the grocery bar*.

devour:
quinoa crepe
slow rendered duck breast
  with beet greens
roasted beets with goat cheese ravioli
chocolate fig cake with
  coconut ice cream

the islands

caribbean
opened in 2001. chef: derrick williams
owners: marilyn reid and shawn letchford
$: cash only
lunch. dinner. reservations recommended

> e38

so you've spent the day at the brooklyn museum support-
ing the arts and now you are famished. walk half a block to
the islands for some "roots and culture" – caribbean style.
if you're lucky, sit at the counter (normally, the lines are
out the door for takeout) and watch as the jamaican chefs
marilyn and shawn prepare all the hits, made to order right
there in their tiny kitchen or eat in the tropical aerie above.
pinch me. i'm back at runaway bay or my nana's kitchen.

imbibe:
sorrel
lemonade

devour:
curried vegetables
rice & peas
garlic shrimp
jerk lamb
shepherds pie

360

modern alsatian cuisine with global influences
opened in 2003.   chef: william brasile. owner: arnaud heart
$$: cash only
dinner. reservations required

> **e39**

before i made my first foray down van brunt, my friend nicole told me about *360* and their support of small farms, particularly greens from redhooks' own *added value*. arnaud and william like to know who grows the ingredients that they use at *360*. take this committment and mix it with modern french cuisine that also pays homage to arnauds' alsatian, italian and north african heritage. with my red hook hosts carolina and john, i happily explored the prix fix menu and the staple seared flanksteak.

imbibe:
organic wines by the glass

devour:
added value field greens
prix fixe menu
roasted cloonshee farm chicken with
  fregola sarga, braised carrots & olives
braised pasture raised rabbit

tuller premium food

cheese and specialty foods
opened in 2002. chef: liam maloney. owner: robert tuller
$$: all major credit cards

> e40

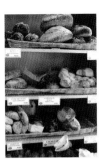

premium, indeed. great lengths (and frequent-flier miles) are taken to insure that in every area of *tuller premuium food* the best of the best is represented. i guarantee you'll discover new brands to invigorate your cupboards. i know a few chefs who come here to discover inspirational ingredients on a regular basis. robert leads a knowledgable staff ready to guide or recommend and liam's prepared dishes keep the neighborhood well fed. i over-heard one customer waxing on and on about the roast chicken. more than a compliment, this was a love poem.

imbibe:
blood orange juice

devour:
ricks's picks specialty pickled vegetables
rotisserie chicken
glorious selection of cheeses
selection of the best breads baked in nyc
regula's specialty cakes
il laboratorio del gelato

two little red hens

an american bakery
opened in 1994. chef / owners: mary louise clemens and christina winkler
$$: all major credit cards accepted
first come, first served

> **e41**

as i approach *two little red hens* bakery, i am drawn in by the sweet aroma of butter and sugar permeating the neighborhood. it's intoxicating: must have cake, must have cake, must have cake now! all baking is done on the premises, 24/7. mary louise and christina have created a cozy kitchen-nook environment in which to present their gorgeous treats. craving a layer cake and it's not your birthday? have a beautifully decorated four-inch individual cake – just enough for one or maybe two!

imbibe:
iced coffee

devour:
brooklyn blackout cake: dark chocolate
   cake, chocolate pudding & fudge frosting
layered birthday cakes
tarts & pies
four-inch individual cakes
cupcakes

85

willy bee's

family lounge with vegan and organic choices
opened in 2004. chef: anya bronsema. owners: serena siegfried and evan zilko
$: mc. visa
breakfast. lunch. dinner. brunch. happy hour. first come, first served

> *e42*

willy bee's is a serious addiction for the five-and-under set and their chaperones. many come here two, three, four times a week and at certain times, the stroller gridlock rivals the brooklyn-battery tunnel. but that's ok — have a latte, take a load off. after a mini grilled cheese or pb & j sandwich, kids roam and mingle in the playroom or garden while dazed parents re-group and re-fuel with espresso milkshakes. beyond the comfort foods, serena and evan also offer tasty vegan and organic choices.

imbibe:
espresso milkshakes
egg creams

devour:
mini grilled cheese
gone fishin' tuna salad with frito scoops
goat cheese quesadillas
pb & j sandwich
real old-fashioned ice cream parlor sundaes

zebulon

neighborhood bar and café with nightly concerts
opened in 2004. owners: guillaume blestel and jef soubiran
$: amex
brunch. late night. full bar. live music. first come, first served

> *e43*

here's the deal: you'll be hard pressed to find a better jazz bar in any borough. *zebulon* is an inviting space, a real collaborative musicians' haven and a great bar. guillaume and jef (the force behind *casimir*) keep it simple: great staff, full bar, free live eclectic music, savory niblets and a wicked vinyl collection. a few words on the savory niblets: snacks like the saucisson, radish bowl, charcuterie plate, oysters, panini — we're not talking goldfish here. c'est radical! coming soon: *this is it: live from zebulon volume one.*

imbibe:
the *zebulon*: shot of dark rum with orange
   slice, rimmed with brown sugar & coffee
wines by the glass

devour:
charcuterie plate
saucisson plate
salad niçoise
prosciutto panini

shop

eat.shop.brooklyn. *first edition*

eat.shop.brooklyn. was researched, written and photographed by agnes baddoo
the eat.shop.guides were created by kaie wellman

top fourteen things that i bought or devoured in brooklyn (or wished i had)

eat

1 > flourless chocolate cake at diner

2 > baked fontina with foccaccio at st. helen café

3 > charcuterie planche at zebulon

4 > my perfect prosciutto sandwich at d'amico's

5 > octopus soppressato with tuna salami at locanda vini e olii

6 > mojito and fish parcel at i-shebeen madiba

7 > arugula, parmesan and bacon salad at acqua santa

shop

1 > dries van noten lace-up flats at butter

2 > agelio batle agave graphite object at matter

3 > stealyourface t-shirt at addy & ferro

4 > kiliwatch side-button sailor shirt at about glamour

5 > carved wood cart at darr

6 > vintage silk ikat robe at umkarna

7 > ysl blouse at fluke

my favorite place to lay my weary head in brooklyn

62-s6 guesthouse

62 south 6th street. corner of wythe. williamsburg
1.718.486.5919
www.62south6.com / dr-cow@myway.com
proprietors: veronica schwartz and pablo castro

highlights >
stylish guesthouse. internet access in the rooms. seven rooms. organic breakfast
(at extra cost).

cost >
low: $85 double with shared bath and shared living room

notes on brooklyn lodging:

there are numerous b&b's in brooklyn, many of them decorated in the victorian style.

for traditional hotels, your best bet on the brooklyn side is the
marriot at the brooklyn bridge.

all rates are for one night. taxes are not included in these rates. please contact the
guesthouse directly for the most up-to-date rates and specials.

about glamour

103 north 3rd street. between berry and wythe. l train: bedford
718.599.3044 www.aboutglamour.net
daily noon - 9pm

vintage men's and women's clothing, livingware, gallery and salon
opened in 2003. owner: shiho aoki
all major credit cards accepted
seasonal sales

williamsburg > 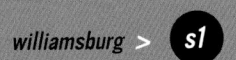 **s1**

i'd been thinking about presents for my goddaughter ama when i wandered into *about glamour*. i went into sensory overload. can there ever be too many things you like under one roof? eyes darting, head turning, i had to take a deep breath and remember, this isn't an olympic competition; i'll have until closing to shop. japanese stationery fills the shelves – folders, notebooks, stickers and an entire shelf of printed cellophane tape! and shiho carries muji, making this shop the only other place in the u.s. other than moma that does.

covet:
muji everything
vintage sailor shirts
printed cellophane tapes
japanese stationery
vintage vivienne westwood
handmade buttons
kiliwatch everything

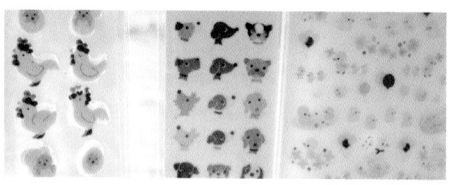

acorn

323 atlantic avenue. between hoyt and smith. a / c / g train: hoyt-schemerhorn
718.522.3760 www.acorntoyshop.com
tu - sa 11am - 7pm su noon - 6pm

handcrafted toys that inspire
opened in 2004. owner: diane crespo and karin schaefer
visa. mc
half-yearly sales

boerum hill >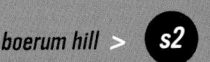

acorn appeals to the child in all of us. they carry the type of toys that spark the imagination and that kids want to play with forever. kids keep these special toys on bookshelves as they grow up and take them with them even when they move out. there's carved wooden figures and puzzles, papier mâché produce for the "farmers market," beautiful artwork, crocheted figures and slippers and a choice selection of clothes. this is the type of place that you come to buy a present and you can't help but buy something for yourself.

covet:
eliza gran
bentley road
brycewear boys' clothes
brooklyn artist ida pearl
mossy creek
makie

addy & ferro

672 fulton street. between south portland and south elliot. a / c train: lafayette
718.246.2900 www.addyandferro.com
m - f noon - 8pm sa 11am - 8pm su noon - 7pm

brooklyn's most eclectic men and women
opened in 2005. owner: erica hutchinson
all major credit cards accepted
seasonal sales

fort greene >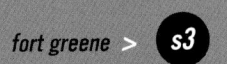

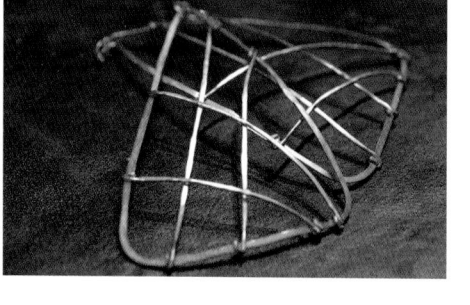

when you walk into *addy & ferro*, there's a t-shirt that reads: develop don't destroy. erica is doing her part developing local talent, not destroying dreams. this is one of brooklyn's most eclectic shops. it's a grand parlour with a back garden where kids can play, so shopping can go on uninterrupted. the assortment of men's and women's clothing and accessories is hip and comfortable, funky and wearble. i found items here i'd seen in passing and wished i owned. now i know where to find them.

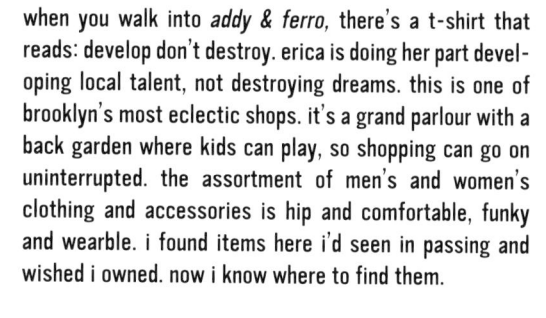

covet:
anu oxidized brass
sistahs of harlem
motif 54
yard
catch a fire by cedella marley
spyoptic eyewear
coup d'etat
oyin handmade hair & body products

amarcord

223 bedford avenue. between north 4th and north 5th. l train: bedford
718.963.4001 www.amarcordvintagefashion.com
daily noon - 8pm

high-end european vintage
opened in 2002. owners: marco liotta and patti bordoni
all major credit cards accepted
half-yearly sales

williamsburg >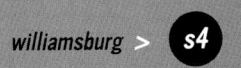

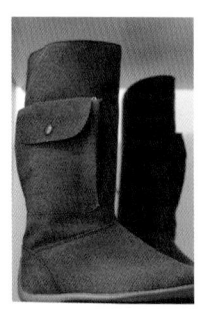

i remember the first time my friend shaheen came thrifting jp (then her friend, now her husband) and me. she quickly learned there is no browsing or meandering. if finding cool gear were a sport to medal in, jp would get the gold. and our favorite spot for fine european vintage shopping is *amarcord*. when i shop here, my heart races and i know – it's on! chic, timeless men's and women's european classics, designer and not are all to be found at *amarcord*. this is the crème of its kind.

covet:
ysl mens & womens
rare european military wear
staggering collection of italian après-ski wear
vintage hermès, dior & gucci ties & bags
sonia rykiel
lacoste
pucci
ungaro

area yoga & baby

252 smith street. between douglass and degraw. f train: bergen. 718.246.9453
m - th 11am - 7pm f - su noon - 8pm
area emporium and spa: 281 smith street. 718.624.3157
www.areabrooklyn.com

yoga and baby
opened in 2004. owner: loretta gendville
all major credit cards accepted
seasonal sales

carroll gardens > **s5**

yoga? babies? in this day and age it almost seems like one begets the other! it did at *area yoga and baby*, originally a store of yoga clothes that by popular demand grew to include a great selection of cute everyday wear for babies and toddlers as well as some choice pre- and post-natal products. the result is a mother and child reunion vibe going on. one-stop shopping for moms and their young kids. i mean, why not? lucky fish t-shirt for me, lucky fish t-shirt for you.

covet:
bobo brooklyn appliqué t's
under the nile cotton printed t's
kiwi industries animal screen t's
lucky fish everything
adult graphic boys shirts
yoga clothes & accessories for adults
blah blah old-fashioned sock dolls
area emporium & spa for the body beautiful

babybird

428 7th avenue. between 14th and 15th. f train: 7th
718.788.4506 www.shopbird.com
m - sa 10:30am - 6:30pm su noon - 6pm

cool, unique baby gifts and hard-to-find toddler designs
opened in 2002. owner: jennifer mankins
all major credit cards accepted
seasonal sales

park slope > **s6**

start 'em young, that's what i say. *babybird* is the off-spring of *bird*, next door. this time for infants to six year olds, jennifer brings the classics, the straight forward, good quality, what-you-want-to-wear-everyday clothes for children. there is a sprinkling of the cutesy, frilly and frothy, but for the most part, you'll find classics like makie and a wide selection of petit bateau twill pants and sailor stripe shirts, with a few quirky clever pieces like monsters with sideburns t-shirts.

covet:
makie
petit bateau
splendid
trumpette
rock t's
matt walker
paulina quintana
monsters with sideburns t's

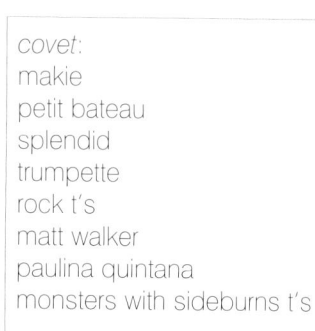

bird

430 7th avenue. between 14th and 15th. f train: 7th
718.768.4940 www.shopbird.com
m - sa 11:30am - 7:30pm su noon - 6pm

chic and sassy women's clothing and accessories
opened in 1999. owner: jennifer mankins
all major credit cards accepted
half-yearly sales

park slope > **s7**

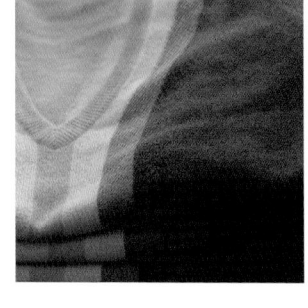

this is the neighborhood shop where you find chic every-day clothes. you know, nothing too dressy or fancy, just beautiful and interesting tops, sweaters or accessories to invigorate jeans, cords and skirts. maybe you're lust-ing for a comfy well-cut dress to throw on? *bird* has this covered. there's an effortless mix here of newer local designers with the beloved and established classics. where beyond madison avenue will you find sonia rykiel sweaters, socks and knit baubles? *bird*.

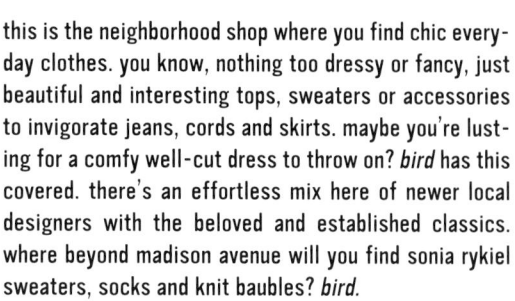

covet:
sonia rykiel sweaters & socks
grey ant
caitlin mocium booklyn-based originals
bing bang lockets & charms
wendy mink
lee angel bronze leaf earrings
soixante neuf turquoise bead charm bracelet
selection of c&c t's

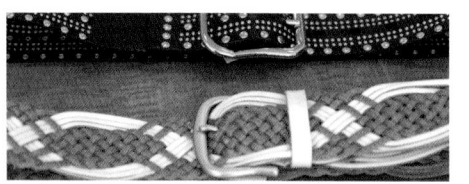

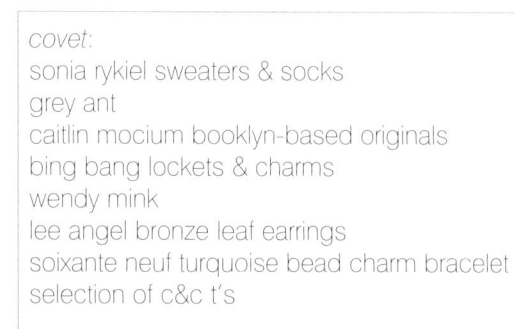

brooklyn collective

198 columbia street. between sackett and degraw. f / g train: carroll
718.596.6231 www.brooklyncollective.com
th - su 1pm - 9pm

artisan collective featuring anything handmade by local artists
opened in 2004. owners: tessa phillips and rachel goldberg
mc. visa

columbia street waterfront district > **s8**

while researching this book, i had several magical brooklyn moments. the late afternoon i spent on columbia street with rachel and tessa was one of the first. in a summer of record humidity, this day was more autumnal: warm, dry and breezy. by chance, i hopped off the bus and happened upon *brooklyn collective's* bi-monthly party in honor of the artists featured, showcasing jewelry, clothes, photography, paintings and silkscreens. it was a block party; neighbors and friends streamed in, all to support local talent.

covet:
rachel goldberg jewelry
samuel peltz photographs
tessa phillips clothes
milton carter silkscreen t's & totes
akari inoguchi
jordan kraft
species by the thousands

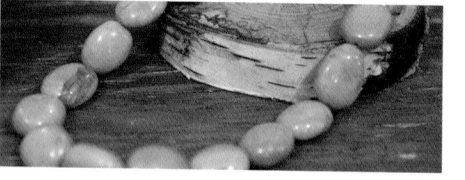

brooklyn general barber emporium

144 bedford avenue. corner of 9th. l train: bedford
718.486.3777
daily noon -8pm

haircuts and cheap thrills
opened in 2004 owner: meredith chesney
cash only

williamsburg >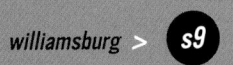

the name says it all. brooklyn, that's right. williamsburg, to be exact. general as in universal, wide ranging, all-purpose barber and emporium. you probably haven't seen such a variety of old-fashioned penny candies and toys since you were down by the shore. for a great price at *brooklyn general barber emporium,* you can get a classic trim and shave in an old-fashioned chair (or mini-plane), listen to bluegrass and country, then pick up a bag of marbles, some rock candy and a handful of mary janes.

covet:
damn fine haircuts
bicycle bell
mary janes candy
old-fashioned candy
monster trucks
marbles
jacks
groovy toys

butter

389 atlantic avenue. between hoyt and bond. a / c / g train: hoyt-schemerhorn
718.260.9033
m - sa noon - 7pm su noon - 6pm

carefully selected designer clothing
opened in 1999. owners: eva and robin weiss
all major credit cards accepted
half-yearly sales

boerum hill >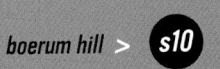

let's start with the name: *butter*. mmmm, yes. if this store existed when i lived on bergen street, i don't think i would have ever crossed the bridge. whatever for? eva and robin have all of my major fashion food groups right here on atlantic avenue: martin margiela, henry beguelin, dries van noten, marni – this place is a fiender's paradise. it is everything that's good about fashion: impeccable crafts-manship, wearability and a chic timelessness that defies trends. butter *is* a food group after all, right?

covet:
dries van noten
rosamaria
rick owens
martin margiela
gary graham
marni
clue t's
henry beguelin

23

calabar imports

820 washington avenue. between lincoln and st. john. 2 / 3 train: eastern parkway
718.638.4288 www.calabar-imports.com
daily 1pm - 9pm

exotic handmade and imported clothes, jewelry and home décor from around the globe
opened in 2004. owners: heloise and atim oton
all major credit cards accepted
seasonal sales

prospect heights > 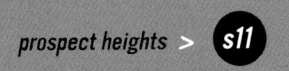 *s11*

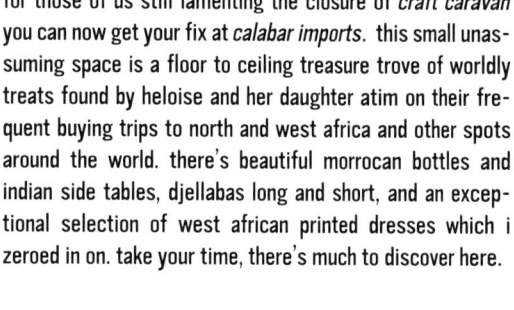

for those of us still lamenting the closure of *craft caravan* you can now get your fix at *calabar imports*. this small unassuming space is a floor to ceiling treasure trove of worldly treats found by heloise and her daughter atim on their frequent buying trips to north and west africa and other spots around the world. there's beautiful morrocan bottles and indian side tables, djellabas long and short, and an exceptional selection of west african printed dresses which i zeroed in on. take your time, there's much to discover here.

covet:
moroccan bottles
indian side tables
long & short djellabas
indian bedspreads
west african printed dresses
i love my hair t's
lanterns

catbird

390 metropolitan avenue. corner of havemeyer. l train: lorimer, g train: metropolitan
718.388.7688 www.catbirdnyc.com
m - f 11am - 9pm sa - su noon - 8pm

focus on eclectic local clothing and jewelry designers
opened in 2004. owners: rony vardi
all major credit cards accepted
seasonal sales

williamsburg >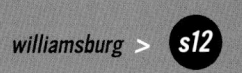

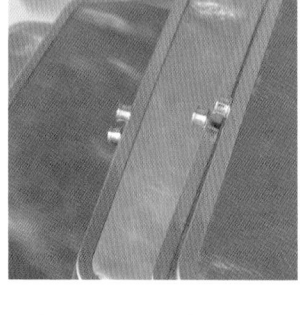

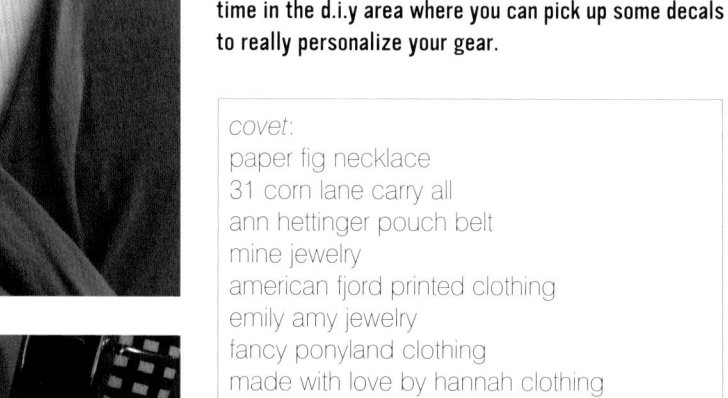

with an eye towards promoting customer individuality rony sifts carefully through the offerings available to bring the best and least exposed clothing and accessories of both established and up and coming designers. the selections at *catbird* don't harken back to any historical era – it's all about the now. look for unique items to update or invigorate your wardrobe and spend a little time in the d.i.y area where you can pick up some decals to really personalize your gear.

covet:
paper fig necklace
31 corn lane carry all
ann hettinger pouch belt
mine jewelry
american fjord printed clothing
emily amy jewelry
fancy ponyland clothing
made with love by hannah clothing

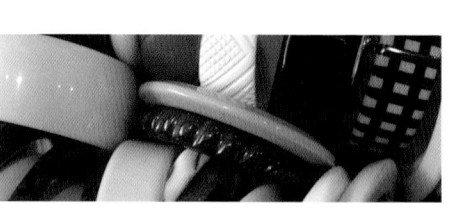

citizen:citizen

248c north 8th street. between roebling and havemeyer. l train: bedford
718.387.1296 www.citizen-citizen.com
m - f 11am - 6pm sa by appointment only

modern minimalist showroom spotlighting progressive u.k. designers
opened in 2004. owners: nicole patel, sweetu patel and philip wood
all major credit cards accepted

williamsburg >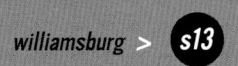

a little off the beaten path, this minimalist space showcases innovative and progressive u.k. designers. *citizen:citizen* is modern, spacious and bright – all the better to contemplate the designers' takes on form and function. you may have hated school but never the desks, remember? their pleasing practicality can't be denied, especially when they're reinterpreted in metal alloy. everything here is inspirational, amusing and organic sleek. with their thoughtful curating nicole, sweetu and phillip have created an intriguing world under one roof.

covet:
fredrikson + stallard >
  table #2
  brush #1
  ming vase
  coat hooks
jimmy st james
  based upon my school desk

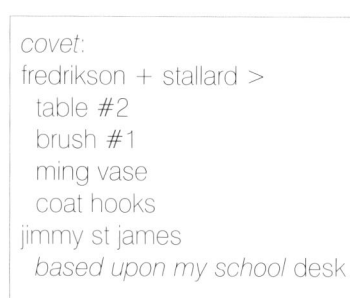

city joinery

20 jay street, 2nd floor. corner of plymouth. f train: york
718.596.6502 www.cityjoinery.com
m - f 9am - 6pm weekends by appointment only

contemporary furniture using traditional techniques and innovative design
opened in 1995. owner: jonah zuckerman
all major credit cards accepted
once-yearly showroom sample sale

dumbo >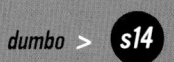

back in the nineteen hundred and eighties there were plenty of designers in nyc, but dumbo was a desolate wasteland. now, down-under-the-manhattan-brooklyn bridges-overpass is buzzing with activity, construction, bike tours and *city joinery*. in a loft overlooking the waterfront, jonah designs handsome contemporary furniture using traditional woodworking techniques. there is a sleek, sweeping gesture to his designs that reminds me of the two bridges stretched outside.

covet:
hovering beds
leaning shelves
woodear end tables
hovering consoles
hewn chairs & dining tables
woven chairs
reading chairs

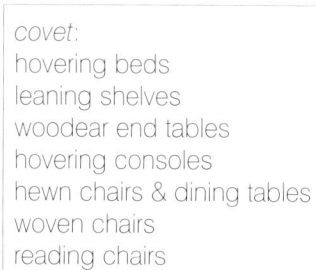

31

cloth

138 fort greene place. between hanson and lafayette
a/c/g train: clinton-washington
718.403.0223
w - su noon - 7:30pm

cozy, contemporary neighborhood shop
opened in 2004. owner: zoë zandewiele
all major credit cards accepted
seasonal sales

fort greene > **s15**

tucked in the ground floor of a brownstone, *cloth* is cozy and appealing. from the first time i passed by last winter, i wanted to shop here. the emphasis is high on quality, low on fussiness; it's organic, earthy and current. there is no re-invention of the retail wheel here, it's just everyday clothes you won't see on everybody else. as if that weren't enough to recommend it, *cloth* is the kind of environment where men comfortably shop for the ladies in their lives. now that's no mean feat.

covet:
billy kirk leather accessories
nili lotan clothing
loomstate organic jeans
brickhouse bath salts & body scrubs
matta, ny bags

cog & pearl

190 5th avenue. between union and sackett
r train: union street, 2 / 3 train: bergen street
718.623.8200 www.cogandpearl.com
w - sa noon - 8pm su noon - 6pm

eclectic mix of handmade items and one-of-a-kind pieces for the home and body
opened in 2002. owners: kristin overson and seth walter
all major credit cards accepted
seasonal sales

park slope > *s16*

when you need a special gift or something to give your home or jewelry box a little love visit *cog & pearl*. with its bright and airy interior decorated with cool soothing colors, you'll feel like you've left the madhouse outside the door. *cog & pearl* focuses on locally made imaginative home items like ceramic mugs, pottery vases, china dishware, glassware, bowls from re-molded vinyl records and serving trays from street signs and delicious jewelry and clothes. waste not want not in full effect.

covet:
john derian decoupage under glass
christina cherry ceramics
alex marshall ceramics
bon bon oiseau jewelry
kim white car upholstery totes
liza mclaughlin jewelry
valerie galloway photography mirrors
faune yeurby artwork

commune salon & gift

191 grand street. between bedford and driggs. l train: bedford, m / j / z train: marcy
718.384.7412 www.communeinternational.com
tu - sa 11am - 8pm su 11am - 6pm

hair salon and gifts
opened in 2004. owner: aki serita
all major credit cards accepted

williamsburg >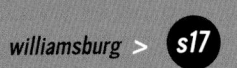

i've never understood the appeal of bustling, crowded, beehive-like hair salons. i don't like to "go where everybody goes" or, more importantly, be seen by everybody every time i go. *commune* is the opposite of that, a calming, spacious loft, with thoughtful retail in front and a low-key salon in back. natural elements are highlighted: a tree branch clothing rail, white feathers suspended from the ceiling, butterflies on driftwood, speakers hidden inside gourds. that's what i call organic modern.

covet:
commune clothes
jewelry>
   masumi okoyama
   yayoi forest
   ema takahashi
instruction in the art of the kimono
japanese camellia hair oil

darr

369 atlantic avenue. between hoyt and bond. a / c / g train: hoyt-schemerhorn
718.797.9733 www.shopdarr.com
tu - sa 11am - 7pm su noon - 6pm

exceptional objects, furniture and new / old stuff we like
opened in 2003. owners: hicham benmira and brian cousins
all major credit cards accepted

boerum hill > 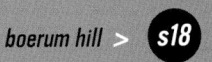 *s18*

darr means home in arabic. in brooklyn, *darr* means exceptional objects and furniture for your home and a gloriously random mix of old and new stuff. through juxtaposition, interior designers hicham and brian give new meaning to even the most ordinary objects. a cluster of vintage perfume bottles, coils of mattress springs, a platter of antlers. it's country, it's modern, it's antique, it was made last week. there's a reason why this is a first stop among production designers in the know.

covet:
wood cart on wheels
antique perfume bottles
wooden bowls
tobacco drying rack
metal transformer covers
antlers
taxidermied birds & animals

826nyc /
brooklyn superhero supply co.

372 5th avenue. between 5th and 6th. f train: 4th-9th
718.499.9884 www.superherosupplies.com / www.826nyc.org
daily 11am - 5:30pm

superhero supply store and non-profit writing center
opened in 2004. executive program director: scott seeley
all major credit cards accepted

park slope > 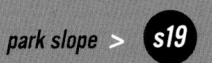 **s19**

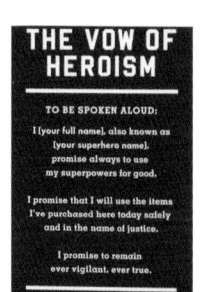

THE VOW OF HEROISM

TO BE SPOKEN ALOUD:

I [your full name], also known as
[your superhero name],
promise always to use
my superpowers for good.

I promise that I will use the items
I've purchased here today safely
and in the name of justice.

I promise to remain
ever vigilant, ever true.

i literally stumbled into this store. i like places that sell things in series: apothecaries, stationery stores, the post office, hardware stores. the *brooklyn superhero supply co.* looked like a hardware store, so in i went. on further inspection, it's closer to bruce wayne's supply store. grappling hooks, capes, cape testers, anti-matter and secret identity kits. kids drag their parents in here pointing out must-have items. this place is ethical commerce at its best: all this fun supports *826 nyc* a non-profit youth tutoring and writing center.

covet:
capes
grappling hooks
particle guns
anti-matter
secret identity kits
oxygen gum

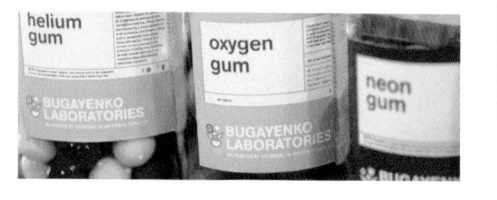

flirt

93 5th avenue. between baltic and warren. 2/3/4/5/n/r train: atlantic. 718.783.0364
252 smith street. between douglass and degraw. f train: bergen. 718.858.7931
www.flirtbrooklyn.com
tu - sa noon - 8pm su noon - 6pm

women's clothing boutiques
opened in 2000. owners: seryn potter, heather falcone and patti gilstrap
all major credit cards accepted
seasonal sales

park slope / carroll gardens > **s20**

imagine that a modern day lucy, ethel and lillian (remember the club election episode?) open a boutique in brooklyn featuring local talent and small labels. lo and behold it does so well they open another. the supportive and mischievious vibe at the *flirt* boutiques draws off the energy and vision of the three owners. one of the huge draws here is the variety of local talent showcased and also the ability to order custom made-to-order skirts – now that's just swell.

covet:
nature vs. future shirt dresses
samoy lenko wrap skirts
house label flirt snap skirts
sound girl corduroy gauchos
custom skirts made to order
3 free wrap dresses
liz anderson cut-out shirts
amy wright tie-front shrugs

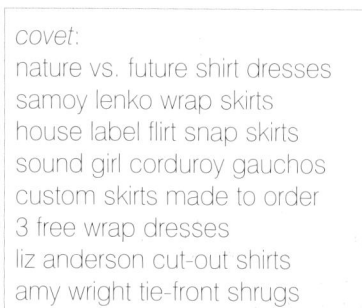

43

fluke

169 wythe avenue. corner of north 6th. l train: bedford
718.486.3166
w - f 1pm - 8pm, su 1pm - 7pm

great vintage, great prices
opened in 2001. owner: caren castleman
mc. visa

williamsburg >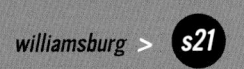

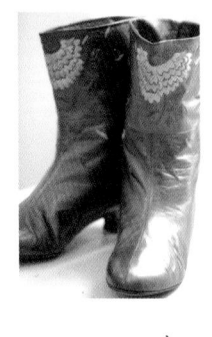

fluke feels like the dressing room suite from a `30s movie — not frou-frou but dreamy. you want to pour a martini, slip on a satin robe and begin shopping. when you are searching for the perfect dress, skirt, shoes or boots, regardless of era, you'll find it here without breaking the bank. there are even some vintage designer pieces slipped into the mix. a variety of flattering dresses are spaciously arranged by color so each piece has room to breathe and reveal its personality.

covet:
raffia dress
ysl blouse
carlos falchi bag
suede lace-up boots
gucci belt

golden calf

86 north 6th street. corner of wythe. l train: bedford
718.302.8800 www.goldencalfnyc.com
tu - su noon - 8pm

chinese and american modern furniture and home accessories
opened in 2005. owner: dennis m. weddle and natalie vichnevsky
all major credit cards accepted
seasonal sales

williamsburg > 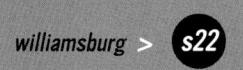 *s22*

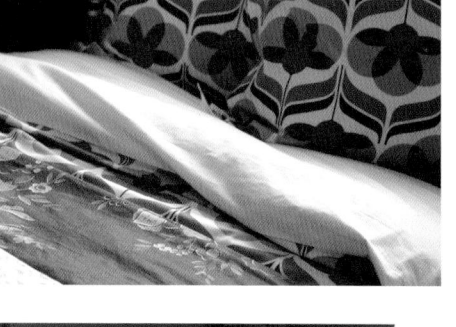

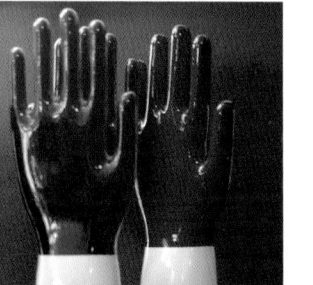

welcome to natalie's world. *golden calf* carries what she refers to as chinese vernacular furniture from the turn of the last century. the late quing period, to be precise. these are not ornate, delicate pieces but sturdy items used in ordinary houses juxtaposed with just enough mid-century modern furniture and bold contemporary patterns to ground you in the now. if repetition is a characteristic of good design, then you can't have enough hall china rubber glove molds lined up to greet you – hi!

covet:
julian hibbard photo jigsaw puzzles
tracing space duvet covers & pillows
chinese vernacular furniture
mid-century furniture
hall china rubber glove molds
wrought-iron antler candlesticks
thomas paul pillows

grdn

103 hoyt street. between atlantic and pacific. a / c / g train: hoyt-schermerhorn
718.797.3628 www.grdnbklyn.com
m - sa 11am - 7pm su 11am - 6pm

practical and stylish products that celebrate the urban gardener
opened in 2004. owner: susanne kongoy
all major credit cards accepted
seasonal sales

boerum hill >

many city people are convinced they have black thumbs. in fact, it's just fear of the unknown. when i lived down the street, *grdn* helped englighten me. susanne inspires and guides the urban gardener with her choice of plants and accessories that are specifically chosen for rooftops, balconies or indoor conditions. problems with your flora? describe the situation to the *grdn* staff and you'll get a solution. and if you still can't deal with growing anything yourself, there's a vibrant mix of cut flowers available.

covet:
natural cotton hemp linens
   by transylvanian images
campo di fiori aged terra cotta pots
guy wolff pottery
parasol hand-blown recycled glass
   humingbird feeders
lightweight fibreclay containers
john derian decoupage paper weights

halcyon the shop

57 pearl street. corner of water. f train: york
718.260.9299 www.halcyonline.com
tu - w noon - 8pm th - f noon - 9pm
sa noon - 8pm su noon - 6pm

better records, more style, less attitude
opened in 2004. owner: shawn schwartz
mc. visa

dumbo >

first i liked *halcyon* because of the mix of technology and nature; bold-shaped patches of indoor grass and stones, wood, metal and colored plexiglass coexisted harmoniously, facing the awesome expanse of the manhattan and brooklyn bridges. *halcyon's* mission is to support and promote all types of underground music, art, fashion. it's a gathering place for beatfreaks and collectors – those in the know and those who want to know more. the idea is to turn you on and keep you coming back.

covet:
electronic house
electro minimal acid
local artist, self published books
local music selection
limited edition prints & t's
hand combed picks by shawn
pro dj accessories
micro designer threads

in god we trust

135 wythe avenue. between north 7th and north 8th. l train: bedford
718.388.2012 www.ingodwetrustnyc.com
m closed tu - su 1pm - 8pm

treasures for men and women alike
opened in 2005. owner: shana tabor
mc. visa
seasonal sales

williamsburg >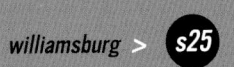

a little bird told me to visit shana's boutique, *in god we trust,* where you can find her line of dresses, coats, blazers and jewelry. there's a sentimental quality, a grandma's parlour feeling to her space with family and pet portraits serving as backdrops. her charm necklaces feel like mementos pieced together from a beloved's jewelry box. shana also offers some vintage pieces and other local designs to round out the offerings — that's how it's done in williamsburg, looking out for one another. amen to that.

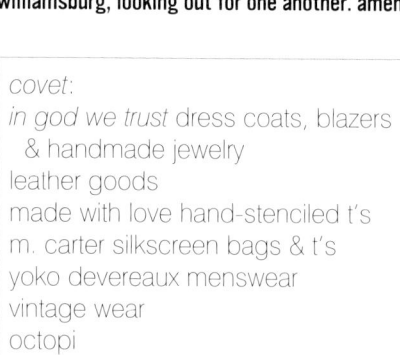

covet:
in god we trust dress coats, blazers
   & handmade jewelry
leather goods
made with love hand-stenciled t's
m. carter silkscreen bags & t's
yoko devereaux menswear
vintage wear
octopi

layla

86 hoyt street. between atlantic and state. a / c / g train: hoyt-schemerhorn
718.222.1933
w - su noon - 6pm

clothes, home and jewelry from india
opened in 2001. owner: alayne patrick
all major credit cards accepted
half-yearly sales

boerum hill > **s26**

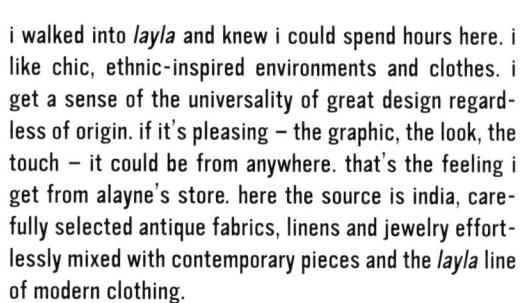

i walked into *layla* and knew i could spend hours here. i like chic, ethnic-inspired environments and clothes. i get a sense of the universality of great design regardless of origin. if it's pleasing – the graphic, the look, the touch – it could be from anywhere. that's the feeling i get from alayne's store. here the source is india, carefully selected antique fabrics, linens and jewelry effortlessly mixed with contemporary pieces and the *layla* line of modern clothing.

covet:
layla clothing
john robshaw bedding & pillows
liwan bedding, sandals & belts
sarah perlis jewelry
pure essential oils
gulab singh oils
megan park homewares

maiden, brooklyn

252 grand street. between roebling and driggs. l train: bedford
718.384.1967 www.maidenbrooklyn.com
tu - su 2pm - 8pm

brooklyn clothes and artist co-op
opened in 2005. owner: radek szczesny
all major credit cards accepted
seasonal sales

williamsburg > 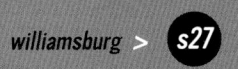 **s27**

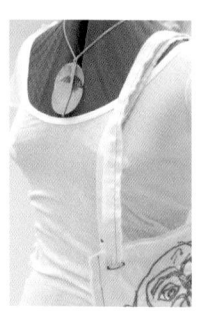

there's a bit of mischief brewing at *maiden, brooklyn* an artist-run storefront and workshop. the punchline of many of these d.i.y designs is seeing the familiar where you least expect it. it's like a friendly guerilla artists' movement. ryan's "shop-dropping project" illustrates this perfectly. he covers ordinary supermarket cans with his own photographs. you may see them here or find them among the canned-goods section at a local supermarket. there might be some slipped in just to bring a smile to your day.

covet:
crash the sky bottle cozies
jackie ross clutches
ryan watkins-hughes photo cans
rainbow-colored decorettes t's
radek's re-claimed t's with
    hand-embroidered phrases

57

matter

227 5th avenue. between carroll and president. m / n / r train: union, f train: 4th
718.230.1150 www.mattermatters.com
tu - sa noon - 7pm su noon - 6pm

graphic objects, books and design resource center
opened in 2003. owner: jamie gray
all major credit cards accepted
seasonal sales

park slope >

matter. something that is being considered or needs to be dealt with. last winter i stumbled upon this designers' mecca. i found many things to be considered and just as many to be dealt with. first on my list: the graphite objects. i'm a fat-nib marker writer and my forays into pencil are of the mechanical kind. i was overjoyed to find this weighty graphite sculpture. it felt so good in my hand, it nearly wrote on its own and it helped me compile a list of books, lighting and glassware that i lusted after.

covet:
a.s. batle graphite objects
alissia melka teichroew diamond rings
mint, nyc ribbon bottle opener
numark portable turntable pt=01
wook kim wallpaper
frank tjepkems gold filigree bling bling
custom furniture design &
   interior consultation

mini jake

242 wythe avenue. corner of 3rd. l train: bedford. 718.782.2005
two jakes: 320 wythe avenue. 718.782.7780
www.minijake.com / www.twojakes.com
tu - sa 11am - 6pm su noon - 6pm

modern kid's store
opened in 2005. owners: david jacobs and inga rogers
all major credit cards accepted
seasonal sales

williamsburg >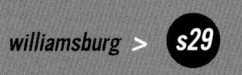

welcome to *mini jake*, a child's world of modern furniture, strollers, bedding and toys. the people behind furniture mecca *two jakes* down the street bring artful, useful and durable child-size things to complement adult pieces. beyond simple designs and excellent quality, there are imaginative mobiles, colorful eva-foam covered pieces and super-light emeco aluminum chairs. furniture can be an investment so why not get cool pieces that go with the rest of your stuff but is also age appropriate?

covet:
maclaren strollers
oeuf bouncers & convertable cribs
bugaboo strollers
haba usa carpets
emeco aluminum superlight chairs
sarah mullins diaper bags
tarantino eva-foam pieces
stokke

mini mini market

218 bedford avenue. between north 4th and north 5th. l train: bedford
718.302.9337 www.miniminimarket.com
daily noon - 9pm

girly bodega featuring local designers
opened in 1999. owners: dana schwister and erika vala
all major credit cards accepted

williamsburg > 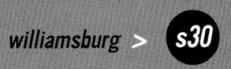 **s30**

mini mini market is the lab for emerging local designers. beyond the wide assortment of clever regional and political t's, many labels here are one-of-a kind items. you'll be certain not to pass anyone on the street in your exact outfit. like any good corner market, there's a little of everything to keep it truly one-stop shopping. handbags, jewelry, vintage shoes, hats, sunglasses, candles. and beware, sometimes there's a wave of happy frenzy as customers find what they didn't know they were looking for.

covet:
mini mini market t's
3-free one-of-a-kind dresses
remix reproduction vintage shoes
superfox jewelry
loop handbags
dolce vita boots
of the sea one-of-a-kind tops

moon river chattel

62 grand street. between wythe and kent. l train: bedford
718.388.1121
tu - sa noon - 7pm su noon - 5pm

architectural salvage, antiques and home furnishings
opened in 1995. owner: christine foley and paul sperduto
all major credit cards accepted

williamsburg > 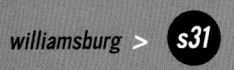 **s31**

no need to beat a trail to new england, there's a general store right here in williamsburg. open since 1995, *moon river chattel* is an discrete institution. you'll find at least one of every basic item that is aesthetically pleasing and functional. through architectural salvage, recaning, rewiring and subtle restoration, paul and christine do their part breathing new life into neglected, well-made items. there's a complementary mix of old and new and a real love of the patina that comes with age.

covet:
america retold home products
soho spices magnetic racks
tea kids clothing
handmade pots from italy
5-cent candy
natural cotton hemp linens from
  transylvania images
rustic wood furniture

65

mor mor rita

218 north 7th street. between driggs and roebling. l train: bedford
718.218.6701 www.mormorrita.com
m closed tu - sa noon - 7pm su noon - 6pm

infant and toddler clothes and accessories
opened in 2004. owner: ryan roche
all major credit cards accepted
seasonal sales

williamsburg > 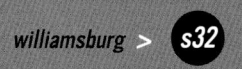 *s32*

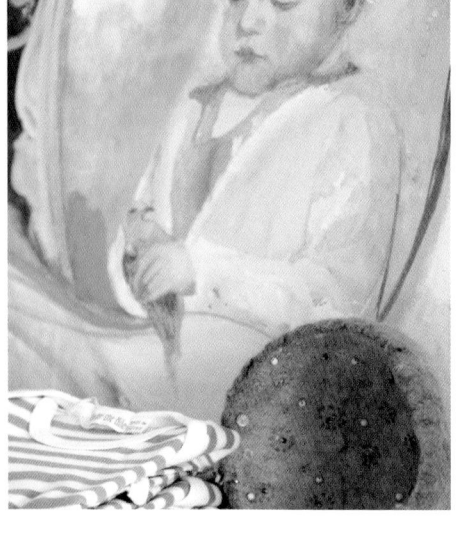

sometimes when i am in a children's store, i wish they made something in my size. at *mor mor rita,* i wish i were a child again. it's the difference between the garment and the time it represents. there is a sweetness, an innocence, a preciousness at this store that reminds me of the sweetness of a baby's breath or the smell of a newly bathed infant. ryan has translated all of that into four walls and an exceptional assortment of new and vintage clothes, toys, china, silverware, jewelry and artwork.

covet:
mor mor rita hand-embroidered t's
  & hand-dyed vintage dresses
souchi cashmere blankets in sorbet
jeanine tasso semi-precious name bracelets
manena frazier hand-sewn bunnies
  & mixed-media paintings
jen sunderland felted animal flowers
antique silver spoons

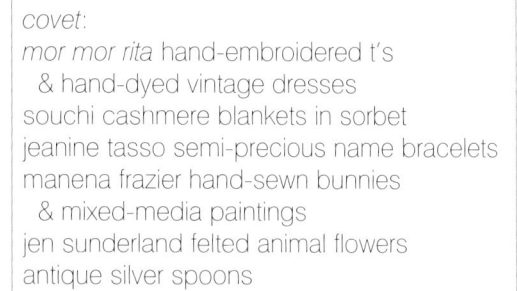

premiumgoods

347 5th avenue. between 4th and 5th. m / n / r / f train: 4th-9th
718.369.7477 www.premiumgoods.net
m - th 1pm - 7pm f 1pm - 8pm sa noon - 8pm su noon - 6pm

sneaker boutique
opened in 2002. owner: clarence nathan iii
all major credit cards accepted

park slope >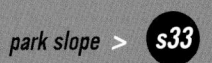

a certain sneaker has already been dipped in gold and displayed at the whitney museum. it won't be long before i receive the sotheby's catalog announcing the auction of someone's collection of unworn, still in the box, first and only limited-edition sneakers – oh, i mean trainers. ladies and gentlemen, start your own collection at *premium goods.* there's every hot-off-the-press, finger-on-the-pulse nike or adidas sneaker, as well as vintage air force ones and jordans. for real.

covet:
vintage air jordans
air force one's
adidas originals
new era
umbro by kim jones
prps

ps9

169 north 9th street. between bedford and driggs. l train: bedford
718.486.6465 www.ps9pets.com
m - f noon - 9pm sa noon - 8pm sun noon - 6pm

holistic pet supplies
opened in 2004. owner: joan christian
all major credit cards accepted

williamsburg >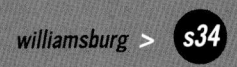

it's been a long time since i've had a dog, but if leo were alive today i'd shop for him here. we love our pets and want the best for them – they are our family. so to get your family member(s) the best visit *ps9* which carries high quality holistic pet supplies presented with humor. there will be none of that fawning, over-protective preciousness for fido or puss here. we all know they just want the important stuff: cool toys, tasty things to eat and gnaw, attractive things to claw and scratch and non-toxic remedies when they're sick.

covet:
ps9 handmade pet beds
artemis pet food
eagle pack pet food
custom pet bowls by local woodworker
around the collar collars
united pet plastic utensils & bowls
homeopathic remedies
shea pet premium skin & coat care

refinery

254 smith street. between douglass and degraw. f / g train: bergen or carroll
718.643.7861
w - sa 11am - 7pm su noon - 6pm

handmade bags
opened in 1997. owner: suzanne bagdade and andrew k. raible
all major credit cards accepted
seasonal sales

boerum hill >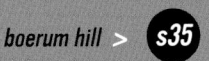

tote bags, make-up pouches, leather wallets, some mother-of-pearl jewelry, and clogs. now you know where to go. they're simple, durable, beautiful and practical all made by hand or made to order. rather than carry a large bag it is always better to distribute the weight – hence the need for many totes in cheerful fabrics. brighten your errands outfit with a new bracelet and some bright colored clogs. not to be left out, are the beautiful hand-tooled leather wallets

covet:
refinery 718 t's
andrew k. raible furniture
suzanne's bags, totes
  & lavender sachets
sven clogs
mother-of-pearl jewelry
vintage children's clothing

saved gallery of art and craft

82 berry street. corner of 9th. l train: bedford
718.388.5990 www.savedtattoo.com
daily noon - 8pm

eclectic boutique and tattoo parlor
opened in 2004. owner: sean mcnanney
all major credit cards accepted
seasonal sales

williamsburg > 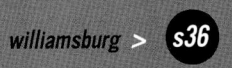 **s36**

there is a certain aesthetic coursing through brooklyn these days. it's part edwardian, part edward gorey and part what i can only call pirate booty. sean is the ringleader; *saved* the epicenter. the recurring image here is the black screened silhouettes of birds, trees and leaves seen on the wallpaper to the fabrics used to upholster the antique furniture. then there's new and vintage clothing, jewelry and striking papier-mâché masks. keep going; the tattoo parlor in back is a true parlor suite fit for blackbeard.

covet:
saved home line wallpapers,
   fabrics & clothing
opening ceremony
in god we trust
antique furniture
contemporary & estate jewelry
bing bang jewelry
thorn jewelry

sleep

110 north 6th street. between berry and wythe. l train: bedford
718.384.3211 www.sleepbrooklyn.com
m closed tu - su noon - 8pm

bedding and lingerie boutique
opened in 2005. owners: amanda grogan and hannah curtin
all major credit cards accepted
seasonal sales

williamsburg > 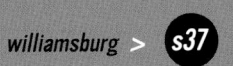 **s37**

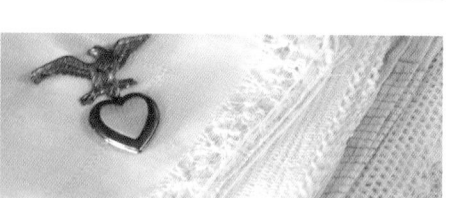

lingerie and bedding have been united at last. throw into the mix luscious lotions, powders, creams and bath products — why ever leave the house after you've made your purchases at *sleep*? amanda and hannah thought of everything to set the mood. ok, so if you have to go out, you know that lingerie isn't limited to slinky stay-at-home wear; there are always foxy foundations. you can wake up, shower, slather on some delicious smelling lotion, slip into yet another something comfortable, and then get dressed to face the day.

covet:
kerry cassil bedding
dwell sets
passion bait
princess tam tam
kai candles, perfumes & lotions
mor cosmetics
estate jewelry
area

sodafine

246 dekalb avenue. between claremont and vanderbilt
a/c train: layfayette or clinton-washington
718.230.3060 www.sodafine.com
tu - sa noon - 8pm su 1pm - 6pm

vintage and handmade clothing, accessories and works on paper
opened in 2005. owners: rebekah maysles and erin weckerle
all major credit cards accepted

fort greene > 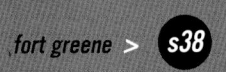 **s38**

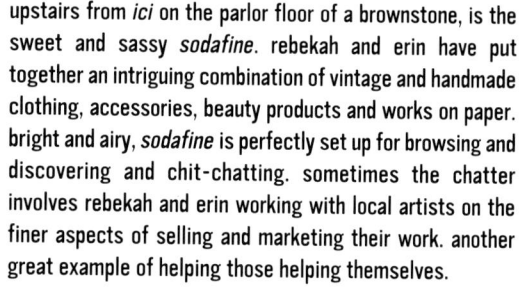

upstairs from *ici* on the parlor floor of a brownstone, is the sweet and sassy *sodafine*. rebekah and erin have put together an intriguing combination of vintage and handmade clothing, accessories, beauty products and works on paper. bright and airy, *sodafine* is perfectly set up for browsing and discovering and chit-chatting. sometimes the chatter involves rebekah and erin working with local artists on the finer aspects of selling and marketing their work. another great example of helping those helping themselves.

covet:
pearl drop handknit/crochet
source book of american chatter zine
feral child clothing
blackberryrose clothing
mellifluoscouture.com
  (reconstructed vintage)
paping zine

spacial etc.

199 bedford avenue. corner of north 6th. l train: bedford
718.599.7962 www.spacialetc.com
m - sa 11am - 9pm sun noon - 8pm

men / women / home: a lifestyle boutique
opened in 1997. owners: janis stemmermann and russell steinert
all major credit cards accepted
seasonal sales

williamsburg >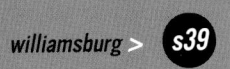

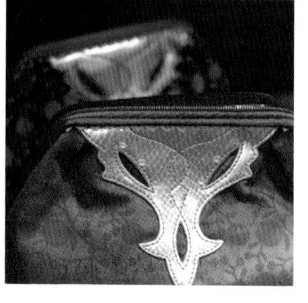

his and hers shoppng, in the same boutique — that's novel. at *spacial etc.* there are great contemporary everyday clothes and accessories to be found, plus beautiful things for the home. sounds like one-stop shopping to me. a silk and cashmere cardigan for her, a jack spade messenger bag for him, pillows, candles and a handsome stainless steel corkscrew for the house. and i love that the owners can think / buy both locally and globally. oh so very modern.

covet:
brooklyn handknit bags, t's
  & bathing suits
wendy mink jewelry
jack spade bags & accessories
spencer peterman wood salad bowls
kikkerland bike repair kits
jill rosenwald ceramic sake sets

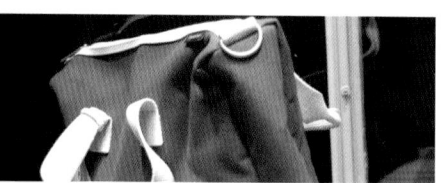

swallow

361 smith street. at 1st place. f train: carroll
718.222.8201 www.swalloglass.com
daily noon - 7pm

handmade things inspired by nature
opened in 1998. owners: ria charisse and anne prosser
all major credit cards accepted

carroll gardens **>**

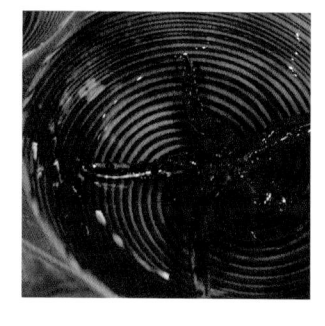

there are stores where you will always find the perfect present, and you hope someone goes there to find something for you. *swallow* is that kind of place. it's a gallery of many types of beautifully crafted handmade things: rainbow vases, sponge coral bracelets, kiln art. all the elements are represented, and everything is made from natural materials: glass, stone, clay, water, paper, silver. you want to hold everything, see how it was made, feel the weight in your hand, take it home.

covet:
kiln art baked enamel jewelry
crystal glaze ceramics
swallow silver rings
silver bird nests by roost
japanese opalescent glass
beaded semi-precious necklaces
excellent card selection
jesse reese

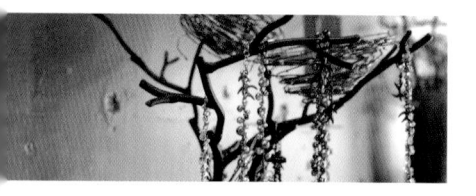

the future perfect

115 north 6th street. corner of berry. l train: bedford
718.599.6278 www.thefutureperfect.com
tu - sa noon - 9pm   su noon - 6pm

design store
opened in 2003. owner: david alhadeff
all major credit cards accepted

williamsburg > 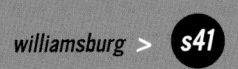 **s41**

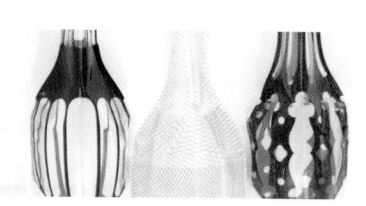

the future perfect is a gallery of whimsical modern furniture, objects, jewelry and art. every which way you turn there are clever functional creations, things you haven't seen before, things you want in your house, things you want to give *and* receive: hand-stitched camouflage chairs, printed plastic vases, rubberband bowls, all kinds of damask wallpaper. my christmas list goes on and on. santa, you know how i've been looking for an interesting coat rack? the ghost tree coat rack will do just fine.

covet:
rubberband bowls
d-bros clear printed plastic vases
heather dunbar hand-stitched
   needlepoint graffiti pillows & chairs
nikolai moderbacher
sarah cihat fifty cent recycled dishes
mt. peters hairy balls
jason miller superordinate antler lighting

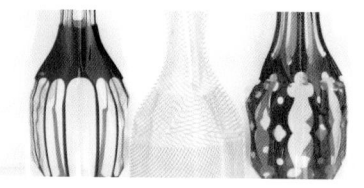

umkarna

69 5th avenue. corner of prospect place
r / d / m / n train: pacific, e / q / 2 / 3 / 4 / 5 train: atlantic
718.398.5888 www.umkarna.com
tu - su 11am - 7pm

clothing, accessories and jewlery manufactured by two women-owned cooperatives in india
opened in 2003. owner: luisa giugliano
all major credit cards accepted
seasonal sales

park slope >

i love the rich colors, sumptuous textures and patterns of indian clothes, textiles and jewelry – new and old. even more i love effecting social change by example. by founding two women-owned cooperatives in india that manufacture the splendid *umkarna* women's, kids' and home accessories, owner luisa has done just that. this is what kaie calls retail activism. i call it ethical commerce. whatever you call it, let's spread the wealth one kurta at a time.

covet:
antique indian textiles & jewelry
umkarna women's & children's clothing
salvor animal t's
antique children's angrahka
jamie joseph jewelry
antique furniture
antique ravi varma prints

87

watts on smith

248 smith street. between douglass and degraw. f train: bergen or carroll
718.596.2359 www.wattsonsmith.com
tu - sa noon - 7pm su noon - 6pm

cool guy classic clothes
opened in 2003. owner: jennifer argenta
all major credit cards accepted
seasonal sales

carroll gardens > 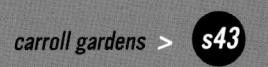 *s43*

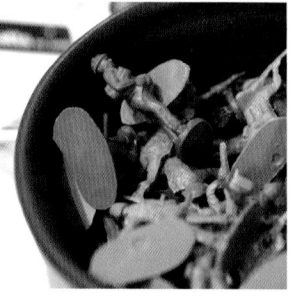

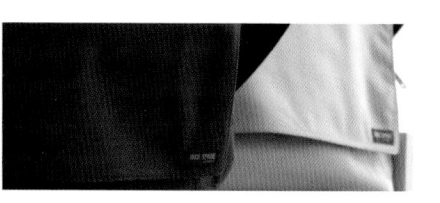

guys need good clothes, too. straightforward, un-trendcon-scious gear with classic lines. i know more and more guys are taking an interest in what they wear, but they still want a shop that's low key and devoid of gimmicks. *watts on smith* is cool haberdashery at its best: paul smith, ben sherman, duffer of st. george – labels known for their quality and timelessness. classic long-and-short sleeved oxford shirts, fred perry polo shirts, vans, jack spade bags – these are all easy pieces to fold into any man's wardrobe.

covet:
paul smith
schiele
trovata
oliver spencer
sacque suit
wrangler
modern amusement
penguin

wonk

68 jay street. between front and water. f train: york
718.596.8026 www.wonknyc.com
daily noon - 7pm

brooklyn-made furniture / design at reasonable prices
opened in 2004. owner: david goltl
all major credit cards accepted
seasonal sales

dumbo >

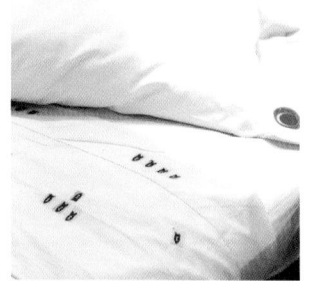

wonk is a showcase for affordable brooklyn-made, mostly modular furniture and lifestyle accessories. with the exception of a couple of tables and chairs, most pieces here have shelves and drawers built into the design somewhere. most pieces are light – in veneer as well as in weight – and are on caster wheels so re-arranging is a snap. with it's simple shapes, thoughtful storage and moveability, *wonk* represents another facet of the dumbo design experience.

covet:
boris tables
mod quad flip-up coffee tables
rubix cabinets
kiln enamel & ceramics
dale kaplan underwear, t's & benchs
greenpoint microsuede benches
  with maple body

woodley & bunny

490 driggs avenue. between 9th and 10th. l train: bedford
718.218.6588
tu - f noon - 8pm sa 11am - 7pm su 11am - 5pm

beauty and lifestyle
opened in 2005. owner: misha and erin anderson
all major credit cards accepted

williamsburg > **s45**

haba, haba, haba. that's short for health and beauty aids, and i can never have enough. soaps, scrubs, bath oils, lotions, creams, conditioners – yes, i do believe pampering is its own regime on a par with yoga and pilates. healthy mind and body, right? at least that's what my mother used to say. hairstylist erin and her sister misha understand this. they've stocked woodley & bunny, this loft-like salon with so much unique, enticing haba and jewelry that you'll be running for a basket to hold your selections.

covet:
trilogy skincare from new zealand
trapp candles
fresh body market
nykaio kenya coffee & sugar scrub
the laundress fabric freshener
mcbrides
foxman silver pendants
mj's herbals

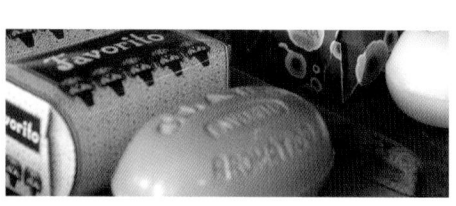